NATIONAL GEOGRAPHIC

Ladders

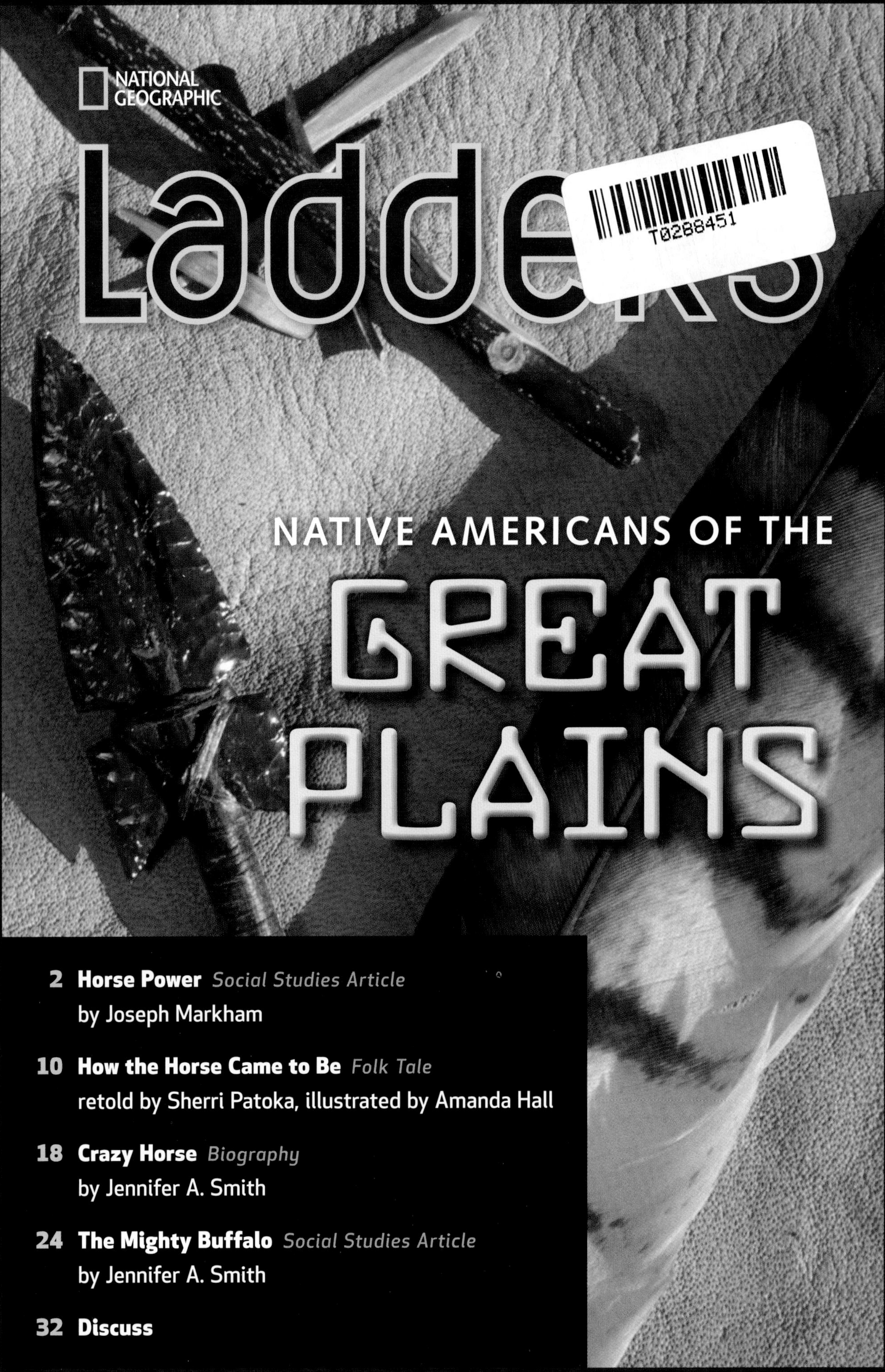

NATIVE AMERICANS OF THE GREAT PLAINS

GENRE **Social Studies Article**

Read to find out how the horse changed Native American history.

HORSE

by Joseph Markham

Cars are important for many Americans. Cars take families where they need to go and help them get things they need, like food. But what was life like before cars?

Early Native Americans of the Great Plains didn't have cars. Often we picture them riding on horseback. However, did you know that people on the Great Plains didn't always have horses?

^ The Lakota people live in the Great Plains. This photo was taken around 1905. It shows two men on horseback wearing feather headdresses. Only the powerful Lakota men wore these headdresses. They earned each feather through special deeds.

The descendants of the horses brought to North America by the Spanish are called mustangs. This wild herd of mustangs is charging through the deserts of Utah.

POWER

When the first Native Americans came to the Great Plains, there were no horses there. Native Americans traveled everywhere on foot or by boat. It took a long time to get from place to place. Therefore, they didn't travel very far.

Then the Spanish arrived in the Americas during the 1500s and brought horses with them. This completely changed life for Great Plains tribes. Let's look at how life with horses was different for them.

TRAVEL

Before the Horse

People have always lived near water so they can drink it, wash in it, and travel on it. Before the horse, early Native Americans traveled on water in boats. They had to move across land on foot. Sometimes it took too long to walk or paddle to places to buy, sell, and trade goods. Instead, people in a tribe would often just share the things they needed. It was easier than trading.

Because it took so long to get around, Plains people usually lived in one area. They used dirt and grass to build homes. They dug part of their home underground to keep it cool in summer and warm in winter.

Sometimes Native Americans had to travel or move farther away. Then tribes loaded their belongings on a travois (truh-VOY), or a kind of sled. Helpful dogs pulled the sleds.

Many Plains Native Americans lived in houses made of dirt and grass when they weren't traveling.

A travois (shown at center below) is a wooden frame that looks like a long triangle. This illustration shows two dogs pulling travois across the plains.

After the Horse

Horses changed the Native Americans' way of life forever. On horseback, they could travel farther and move faster. They could carry much heavier loads. With horses, many tribes of the plains became **nomadic**. They moved from place to place, following herds of buffalo. In late spring and summer, groups of buffalo would stay in one place to raise babies. The tribes would also stop traveling so they could hunt the buffalo herds.

Many Great Plains tribes began to change the way they built their homes to fit their nomadic way of life. A hut could not be moved from place to place easily. Instead, tribes built **tipis**, or tents made of animal skins. A tipi could be moved easily from place to place.

Horses allowed Native Americans to travel more. With a horse, tribes could trade with more people. Horses were also valuable things to trade. Because of this, they became a symbol for wealth. The tribe with the most horses had the most power.

Women were often in charge of setting up the tipis. They created a cone shape with thin wooden poles. Then they wrapped large animal skins around the outside of the cone.

A Native American child rides on a travois. The child sits on a platform resting between two poles that are attached to her mother's horse.

Before the Horse

Buffalo had always been important to Great Plains tribes. Before people had horses, hunting buffalo was especially dangerous. Buffalo roamed the plains in herds. They could **stampede** over everything in their path. Plains hunters had to outsmart the buffalo herds in different ways.

Buffalo do not see very well. Native Americans disguised themselves under skins of buffalo or other animals. Then they snuck up on a buffalo and attacked it. They also surprised buffalo to make them stampede and fall off cliffs. The hunters then used the buffalos to make clothing and tipis. Unfortunately, these tricks all put the hunters in danger.

This painting depicts how some hunters might have hunted buffalo. They wore wolf skins as a disguise. Then they could sneak close enough to the animal to attack it.

After the Horse

With horses, Great Plains hunters used the same hunting methods in faster and safer ways. Horses could run as fast as a buffalo. Hunters could chase the buffalo or flee from them. Native Americans could also follow buffalo across wider areas of land on horses. They could carry more food and water to hunt the buffalo for longer amounts of time.

Native Americans on the Great Plains soon focused on the buffalo for their wealth. Horses made hunting buffalo easier. Tribes suddenly had many buffalo hides to trade for other goods. However, hunting and trading on horseback came with new risks. While hunting or trading, hunters sometimes entered land that belonged to another tribe. That is called trespassing. If they trespassed, fights could break out.

Hunters used their horses to force the buffalo toward their camp. More hunters waited there to attack the buffalo.

On horseback, Native Americans could make a quick getaway if the buffalo turned and stampeded.

ALLIES AND ENEMIES

Before the Horse

Throughout history, tribes sometimes made **allies**, or friends, among other nearby tribes. Other times, they made enemies. Before the horse, tribes living in the same area might be friends. They might share information and the things they needed to live. However, neighboring tribes might also fight over the land and the things they needed.

Before the horse, warriors mostly fought on foot. Small fights broke out sometimes and ended quickly. Larger fights might last longer. Many people on both sides might be hurt or killed during these long battles.

This Native American drawing from 1833 shows a Mandan chief and a Cheyenne chief in hand-to-hand combat. Their tribes were bitter enemies.

ALLIES AND ENEMIES

After the Horse

The horse changed the way tribes lived together. With horses, Native Americans could make friends with tribes that lived farther away. When tribes fought, many other tribes could travel quickly on horseback to help their allies. Because horses made it so easy to get around, having them gave a tribe power. Horses were worth so much that tribes stole them just to hurt their enemies.

Horses allowed Native Americans to trade with new allies. For example, they could ride to new settlements. The Europeans that lived there bought the Native American's buffalo hides and sold weapons to them. The weapons made tribes better warriors and hunters. Horses brought new freedom to the Plains people and allowed them to create these new relationships and trade agreements.

Men of the Crow tribe and other Native Americans trade goods.

Horses did many of the same tasks that dogs did. Some Native Americans called horses "big dogs." There was no word for *horse* in their languages.

Check In How did horses change the way the Native Americans of the Great Plains lived?

GENRE Folk Tale **Read to find out** how the horse came to the Blackfoot people.

How the Horse Came to Be

retold by Sherri Patoka illustrated by Amanda Hall

Native American stories such as this one often include a vision quest. During a vision quest, a person asks a spirit what to do. This story tells how a spirit helps a boy. It also shows how important horses were to the Native Americans of the Great Plains.

The Blackfoot were one of the earliest groups of Native Americans to live on the Great Plains. They were great buffalo hunters. When the Blackfoot got their own horses, their lives changed. This Blackfoot folk tale is a story from the past that is known to many. It will tell you how the Blackfoot first got horses.

Many years ago, a boy named Long Arrow lived with the Blackfoot because his parents had died. He came from a different tribe, so he felt like he didn't belong. He looked and looked for ways to make his life better. Praying did not bring him an answer. Going without food did not bring him an answer. Finally, he went to the plains to search for a sign.

The plains seemed endless to Long Arrow. Long Arrow was so upset that he could not see how beautiful the land was. He grew tired and lost hope. Not knowing what else to do, he stopped beside a lake and began to cry.

Long Arrow didn't know it, but a very old and very powerful Water Spirit lived in this lake. The Water Spirit felt sad for the boy, so he sent his own son to get him. "Go now, my son," he said, "and bring this crying boy to me." The son of the Water Spirit swam up to the surface of the lake and greeted the boy.

"Who are you, and what do you want?" Long Arrow asked in surprise.

"Hurry. Come with me," the Water Spirit's son replied. "I will take you to see my father, the Water Spirit. Hold on to my shoulders, and keep your eyes shut. Do not open them until I tell you to."

Long Arrow held the other boy's shoulders tightly and closed his eyes, and the son of the Water Spirit dove deep into the lake. As they swam down through the water, the boy told Long Arrow what to do. He said, "My father will offer you an animal from the lake. Choose the old duck and her little ducklings." Long Arrow was puzzled by these directions, but he nodded in agreement.

Just then, Long Arrow and the son reached the Water Spirit. "You may open your eyes now," the son said. Long Arrow opened his eyes to see a very old man with long white hair.

"Why are you crying, my boy?" asked the Water Spirit.

"I have only had bad luck," answered Long Arrow. "I am searching for something that will make my life better."

"I will happily help you," said the Water Spirit. "I can give you any animal from this lake. Which animal would you like?"

Right away, Long Arrow replied, "The old duck and her ducklings."

"That duck is so old! Why don't you choose another animal?" the Water Spirit asked.

The Water Spirit tried four times to get Long Arrow to change his mind. Each time, Long Arrow just said, "I will take the old duck and her ducklings."

Finally, the Water Spirit smiled and said, "After dark, my son will catch the duck for you. Then you must take the duck and her ducklings and walk away without looking back."

That night, the Water Spirit's son caught the duck. He tied a piece of braided grass around her neck like a leash. Then he handed the leash to Long Arrow and said, "You must not look back until dawn." Long Arrow walked into the darkness. He could hear duck wings flapping behind him.

Long Arrow walked all night. Soon, he stopped hearing quacking noises behind him. However, he did not look back. Then he began to hear a new noise behind him: "clomp-clomp." Still, he did not look back. Next, the grass leash turned into a thick rope in his hands. Still, the boy did not look back.

Finally, when dawn came, Long Arrow turned around. He did not see a duck behind him, he saw a horse! He rode the horse back to the Blackfoot camp. Behind him, he heard many other horses galloping.

At first, his people were surprised and frightened by the strange beasts. They called the horses "elk-dogs" because they were so big. Long Arrow gave each Blackfoot a horse and let the remaining horses run across the plains.

The Blackfoot people learned how to ride, and how to use the horses to carry their belongings. Horses made many things easier. The Blackfoot could cross rivers easily when riding horses. They could find buffalo herds and chase and hunt the buffalo. The people were happy with the horses and with Long Arrow.

When Long Arrow grew older, the Blackfoot made him a chief because of the wonderful gift he had brought to them. The boy's luck had finally changed!

Check In What rule did Long Arrow have to follow once he accepted the Water Spirit's gift?

GENRE Biography **Read to find out** about the life of a great Lakota chief.

Crazy Horse

by Jennifer A. Smith

A Black Hills Warrior

Even when he was a boy, Lakota chief Crazy Horse did great things. People said he killed his first buffalo by the time he was 12. When he was 16, he saved a friend during a big battle. His actions as a young man showed he would be a great warrior and leader.

Crazy Horse was born around 1842 and lived in the Black Hills of what is now South Dakota. This place has always been **sacred** land to the Lakota tribe, which means it was very special to them. Crazy Horse grew up understanding the importance of the land. For years, his people had lived, fought, and died for it. His love for his land made him brave. Of course he would fight to keep it safe.

The Black Hills are located in South Dakota and Wyoming. They are a small mountain range that rise out of the western Great Plains.

Battle of the Little Bighorn

Native Americans already lived on much of the land out west. However, many settlers came to make a living there. They farmed the land and dug for metal and valuable stones. When the settlers and Native Americans began to fight, the U.S. government tried to end the fights with **treaties**. The treaties were often ignored, however, and the Native Americans and the settlers just kept fighting.

In 1874, Lieutenant Colonel George A. Custer led U.S. Army soldiers onto Crazy Horse's land. They looked for gold and found it. Other people believed they could get rich by finding gold, too. They raced to settle the land during what is called a **gold rush**. As more settlers arrived, more Native Americans and settlers began to fight. Two years later, the government ordered the Native Americans in the area to leave their land and move onto **reservations**.

Artist William Herbert Dunton created this painting. He wanted to show how he imagined the action at the Battle of the Little Bighorn.

Some groups agreed to move, but others joined together to say no. Chiefs such as Crazy Horse, Sitting Bull, and Little Big Man would not go. Crazy Horse organized 1,200 warriors to stop the soldiers who came to make them go. It worked! A week later, about 1,500 Native Americans won a fight against about 650 soldiers led by Custer. More than 200 U.S. soldiers died, including Custer and all the troops he led.

The fight is known as the Battle of the Little Bighorn. It is named after a river that is found nearby. It is also known as "Custer's Last Stand." Custer chose never to give up. Because he did not see how large and powerful the group of Native Americans was, Custer and his men died in the battle. Soon after, the U.S. government forced Crazy Horse to surrender himself to them. Although he had won this battle, he died in a fight with soldiers a little more than a year later.

Lieutenant Colonel George A. Custer made serious mistakes during the Battle of the Little Bighorn. He underestimated the Native Americans' power.

My lands are where my dead lie buried.

—CHIEF CRAZY HORSE

This huge sculpture of Crazy Horse's face was carved with chisels and dynamite. It is part of a larger, unfinished sculpture shown below at right.

This model shows visitors how the sculpture at right will look when it is finished.

Crazy Horse's Legacy

People remember Crazy Horse as one of the greatest Native American leaders ever. He fought to keep his people's lands, but unfortunately the Lakota lost. Today, the Lakota live on reservations that cover only a small part of their sacred lands.

In 1980, the U.S. Supreme Court said that the U.S. government did not have the right to take the Lakota's land. The Court told the government to pay the Lakota for the land. However, the Lakota said they would not take the money and sell the land. Many Lakota who still live on nearby reservations are still fighting to get the land back today. Like Crazy Horse, these people say they will never give up their land.

An artist and a Lakota chief wanted to honor Crazy Horse's life. They raised money to carve the Crazy Horse Memorial on a rocky mountain in the Black Hills. When it is done, this huge sculpture will be the largest mountain carving in the world.

LAKOTA MEDICINE MAN BLACK ELK'S MEMORY OF CRAZY HORSE

"People would find [Crazy Horse] out alone in the cold, and they would ask him to come home with them. He would not come, but sometimes he would tell the people what to do. People wondered if he ate anything at all. Once my father found him out alone like that, and he said to my father: 'Uncle, you have noticed me, the way I act. But do not worry; there are caves and holes for me to live in, and out here the spirits may help me. I am making plans for the good of my people.'"

Check In Why did the U.S. government force Crazy Horse and his people to move onto reservations?

GENRE Social Studies Article

Read to find out why buffalo are important to Native Americans of the Great Plains.

THE Mighty Buffalo

by Jennifer A. Smith

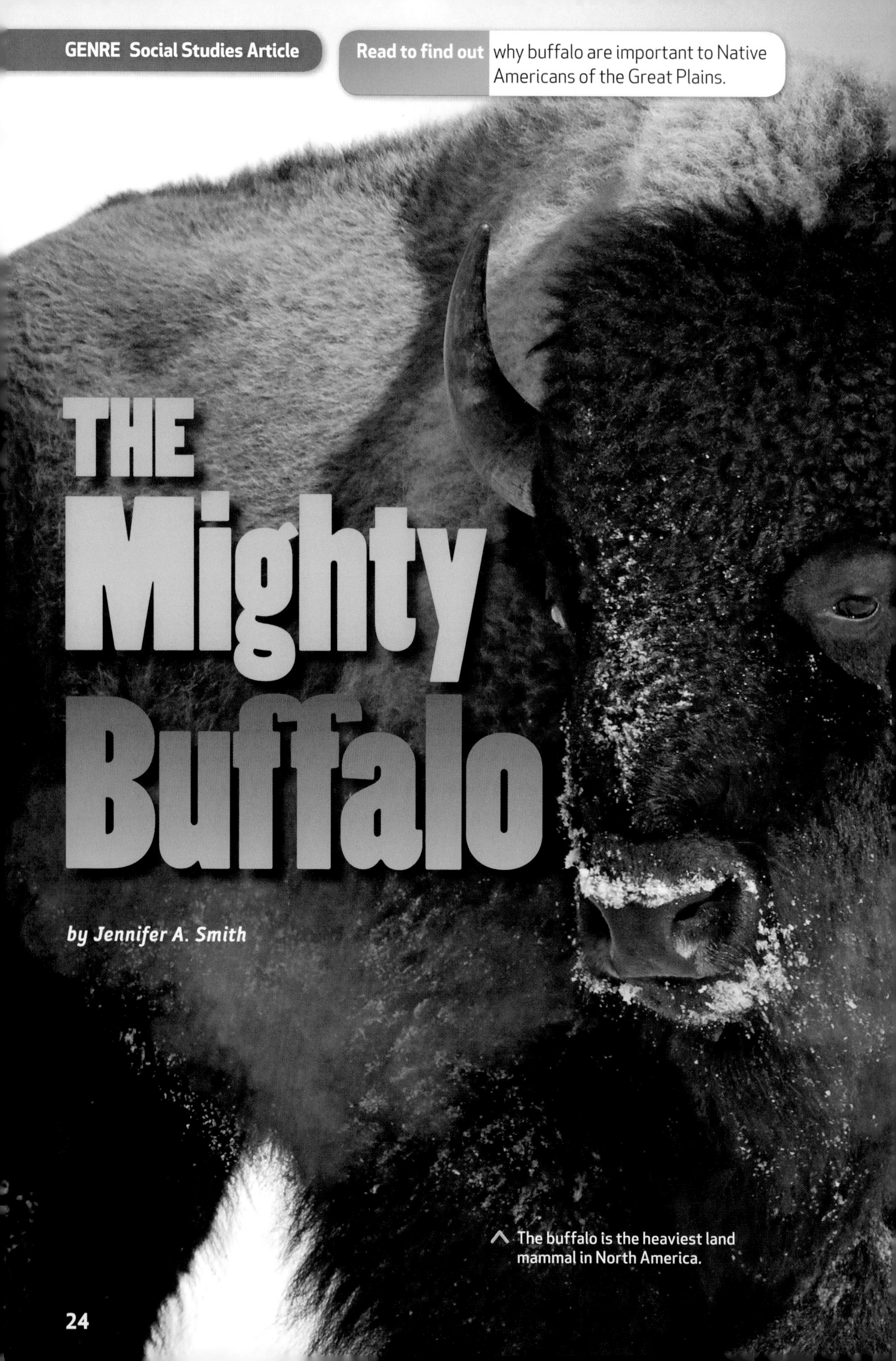

The buffalo is the heaviest land mammal in North America.

A Hairy Situation

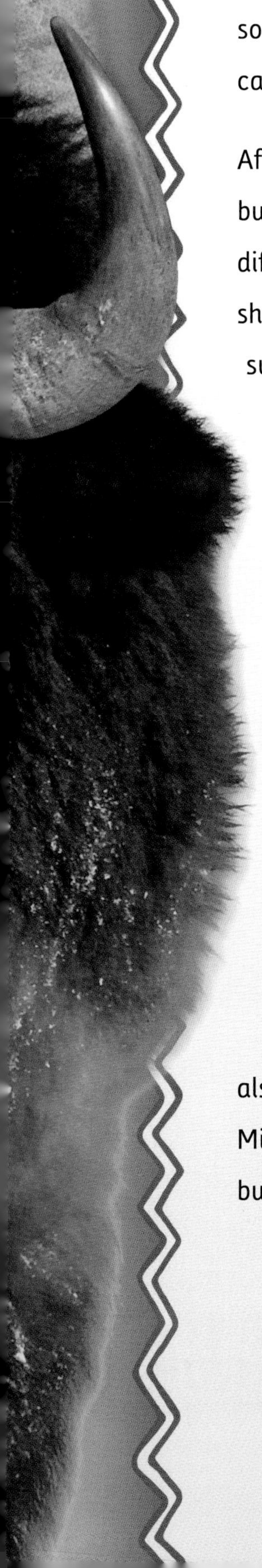

Be careful if you ever meet a buffalo! A male buffalo is taller than an average-sized man. He weighs about 1,800 pounds. He can't see well, so it's easy to surprise a buffalo. Unfortunately, surprising a buffalo can be dangerous.

After noticing his huge size, you will notice the thick hair of a buffalo's mane and beard. A buffalo, also called a bison, has two different kinds of hair. One is long and rough, while the other is shorter and woolly. The two lengths of hair keep a buffalo cool in the summer and warm in the winter. In winter, snow sticks to a buffalo's special hair. The buffalo can shake the snow off before it melts and makes his skin cold.

A buffalo's sharp horns and hooves look dangerous. But buffalo are only dangerous if they think you want to hurt them. Try watching them from far away. Then you can see that they are gentle giants.

At one time, many millions of buffalo roamed throughout the American West. Their hooves made a loud noise as they beat on the ground. Therefore, people nicknamed the buffalo "thunder of the plains." In the mid-1800s, many hunters came west on new railroads. They came to hunt the huge, fast animals for fun. Sometimes they even shot them while riding on trains. Settlers also killed buffalo for food, and traders sold buffalo meat and hides. Millions of these gentle giants were killed, until only a few hundred buffalo were left. They came close to **extinction**.

Remembering the Buffalo

The Plains tribes needed to use the buffalo for clothing, food, and even shelter. Therefore, it was very hard when the buffalo began to disappear. The buffalo gave them everything they needed.

Plains tribes even performed **rituals**, or sacred ceremonies, about the buffalo. For example, they often performed a Buffalo Dance at the beginning of the hunting season. They hoped the dance would help the hunters find the herds. Dancers dressed and moved like buffalo. This dance was an important ritual that showed respect for the animal.

American settlers were killing too many buffalo. However, the U.S. government did not want to stop them. Native Americans could be forced onto reservations more easily if there were no more buffalo to hunt. Without buffalo, there was also no food or skins to trade or make clothing from. Plains people could not meet their own needs anymore, so they gave in and moved to reservations.

In 1883, many Plains tribes held their last buffalo hunt. After that, there were not enough buffalo left to hunt.

Native Americans of the Great Plains made shoes out of animal hides. This pair is made of buffalo.

Plains Indians often recorded important events by painting buffalo hides. This painted hide depicts a dance after a successful hunt.

Buffalo robes kept people warm during the icy winters on the plains.

Buffalo Bill's Wild West Shows

William F. Cody introduced the buffalo to Americans who did not live on the Great Plains. His nickname was "Buffalo Bill," and he got it by winning a buffalo-hunting competition. In just two years, Cody killed more than 4,200 buffalo by himself. At that time, Cody worked for a railroad company. Cody's team was laying metal railroad tracks across the plains. His job was to cook meals for everyone. He fed all of those men with the buffalo he hunted.

In 1883, Buffalo Bill put on his first Wild West shows. The shows explained to people what life was like in the Wild West. They played characters such as cowboys and Native Americans. His show traveled around the United States and Europe for 30 years. Audiences enjoyed watching actors pretend to hunt buffalo. Buffalo Bill became well-known by killing buffalo. However, his Wild West shows helped save the buffalo. They made Americans understand that the buffalo faced extinction.

Native Americans were an important part of Buffalo Bill's Wild West show. However, they had to reenact and lose a battle with "U.S. Army" soldiers each night.

^ Buffalo Bill's Wild West show provided a family-friendly glimpse into life in the American West. It was a popular show in the United States and Europe.

> Before starting his own Wild West shows, Buffalo Bill Cody took part in a staged buffalo hunt for tourists at Niagara Falls.

Custer State Park is in the Black Hills of South Dakota. The buffalo here are protected and carefully looked after to keep them healthy.

Return of the Buffalo

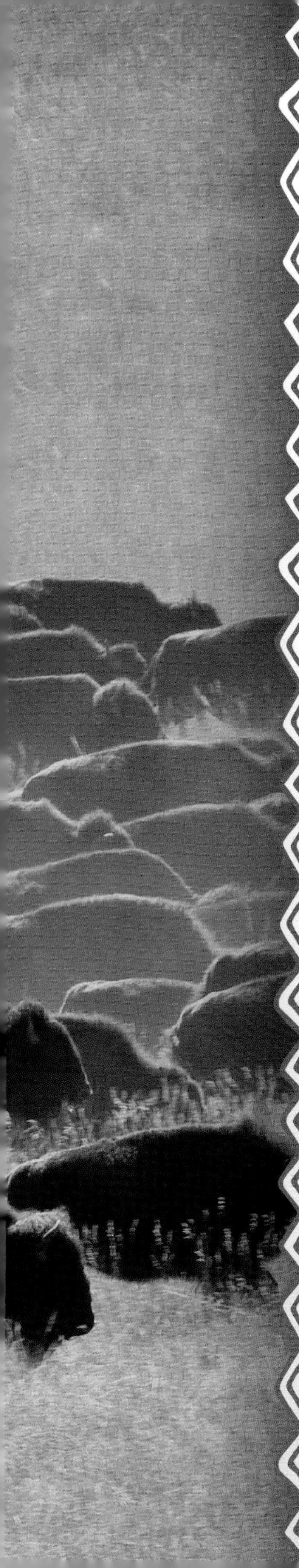

Today, the buffalo is not dying out. Starting around 1900, people began working to conserve, or protect, the land, water, and animals of our nation. This work included saving the buffalo. **Conservationists** got cattle ranchers to raise buffalo. Ranchers sold buffalo for food, but they also sent some buffalo to live on protected land.

In 1908, land in Montana was set aside for buffalo. In this **refuge**, the animals can live safely. No one will hunt them. The National Bison Range is one of the oldest wildlife refuges in the United States. It can hold up to 500 buffalo.

Another project to save buffalo started in Yellowstone National Park, the first national park. Yellowstone is the only place in the country where buffalo have always lived. About 3,000 buffalo live there now, the largest number of buffalo living on public land anywhere. In the park, signs warn visitors to stay far away from the buffalo.

There will never again be millions of buffalo living on the Great Plains. However, the government, conservationists, and cattle ranchers have worked hard. They have saved the buffalo from extinction.

Check In Why was the buffalo important to Native Americans?

Discuss

1. What connections can you make among the four selections in this book? How do you think the selections are related?

2. How does the folk tale of Long Arrow show the importance of the horse to the Blackfoot people?

3. Why do you think Chief Crazy Horse is still remembered by Americans today?

4. Do you think Buffalo Bill was more of a friend or more of an enemy to the buffalo? Why? Support your opinion.

5. What do you still wonder about the Native Americans of the Great Plains and the issues and events that have been important in their history?